Read for a Better World™

TECHNOLOGY

A Look at THEN and NOW

PERCY LEED

GRL Consultant, Diane Craig, Certified Literacy Specialist

Lerner Publications ◆ Minneapolis

Educator Toolbox

Reading books is a great way for kids to express what they're interested in. Before reading this title, ask the reader these questions:

> What do you think this book is about? Look at the cover for clues.
>
> What do you already know about technology in the past?
>
> What do you want to learn about technology in the past?

Let's Read Together

Encourage the reader to use the pictures to understand the text.

Point out when the reader successfully sounds out a word.

Praise the reader for recognizing sight words such as *on* and *the*.

TABLE OF CONTENTS

Technology Then and Now

People are always making new tools.

THEN

Cameras took pictures.

NOW

Phones take pictures too.

THEN

People talked on home phones.

NOW

People make video calls.

THEN

Movies were only in theaters.

NOW

People can watch movies at home.

Have you ever sent a letter?

THEN

People wrote letters.

NOW

People send texts and emails.

THEN

News came in the newspaper.

Where else can you get news?

NOW

Many people get news online.

THEN

Music played on the radio.

NOW

Phones play music too.

THEN

Kids played board games.

NOW

Kids play video games too.

We have many new tools today.

You Connect!

Does your family use any old tools?

How would your life be different without cell phones?

How can you learn more about technology in the past?

Social and Emotional Snapshot

Student voice is crucial to building reader confidence. Ask the reader:

What is your favorite part of this book?

What is something you learned from this book?

Did this book remind you of any tools you use?

Opportunities for social and emotional learning are everywhere. How can you connect the topic of this book to the SEL competencies below?

Relationship Skills
Self-Awareness
Social Awareness

Photo Glossary

camera

newspaper

radio

theater

Learn More

Amstutz, Lisa J. *Before Television*. Lake Elmo, MN: Focus Readers, 2020.

Dinmont, Kerry. *Communication Past and Present*. Minneapolis: Lerner Publications, 2019.

O'Brien, Cynthia. *Technology Then and Now*. New York: Crabtree Publishing Company, 2019.

Index

Photo Acknowledgments

The images in this book are used with the permission of: © Rido/Shutterstock Images, pp. 4-5; © Library of Congress, 6, 14, 23 (camera, newspaper); © praetorianphoto/iStockphoto, p. 7; © Everett Collection/Shutterstock Images, pp. 8, 12, 16-17, 23 (radio); © Ridofranz/iStockphoto, p. 9; © The New York Public Library, pp. 10, 18, 23 (theater); © Sellwell/Shutterstock Images, p. 11; © Rat0007/iStockphoto, p. 13; © Prostock-Studio/iStockphoto, p. 15; © Tatiana Buzmakova/iStockphoto, p. 16; © DjelicS/iStockphoto, p. 19; © fizkes/iStockphoto, p. 20.

Cover Photographs: © Library of Congress (inset); © Prostock-Studio/iStockphoto (tablet)

Design Elements: Mighty Media, Inc.

Lerner Publications Company
An imprint of Lerner Publishing Group, Inc.
241 First Avenue North
Minneapolis, MN 55401 USA

For reading levels and more information, look up this title at www.lernerbooks.com.

Main body text set in Mikado a Medium.
Typeface provided by Hannes von Doehren.

Library of Congress Cataloging-in-Publication Data

Names: Leed, Percy, 1968–author.
Title: Technology : a look at then and now / Percy Leed.
Description: Minneapolis : Lerner Publications, [2024] | Series: Read about the past (Read for a better world) | Includes bibliographical references and index. | Audience: Ages 5–8 | Audience: Grades K–1 | Summary: "We didn't always have phones, computers, and TVs. So what did people do? In this book, photographs from the past give readers a way to see just how different technology used to be"—Provided by publisher.
Identifiers: LCCN 2022037146 (print) | LCCN 2022037147 (ebook) | ISBN 9781728491486 (library binding) | ISBN 9798765603543 (paperback) | ISBN 9781728499505 (ebook)
Subjects: LCSH: Technology—History—Juvenile literature. | Inventions—History—Juvenile literature.
Classification: LCC T48 .L36 2024 (print) | LCC T48 (ebook) | DDC 609—dc23/eng/20221006

LC record available at https://lccn.loc.gov/2022037146
LC ebook record available at https://lccn.loc.gov/2022037147

Manufactured in the United States of America
1 - CG - 7/15/23